Why do we dance?

T0337106

Written by
Sarah Jane Lewis-Mantzaris
Illustrated by Jan Smith

Collins

What's in this book?

Listen and say 🎧①

dance

dancers

Download audio at www.collins.co.uk/839687

music

musicians

Katy says, "Mum, why do Grandma and Grandpa dance?"

Mum says, "That's a good question, Katy. Why do people dance?"

Look at this picture. It is very old.
The people are dancing.

Musicians play music and
dancers dance.

People like dancing.

Some dances tell a story.

This dance is a ballet. The dancer is telling the story of Cinderella.
Do you know this story?

Ballet dancer

In this ballet, a girl, Clara, has got a new toy.

The Nutcracker ballet

People dance when they are happy, too. This is a carnival.

Carnival dancers

People dance in the streets.
Do you like the dancers' clothes?

Lots of people go to dance classes.

A Zumba dance class

People dance with other people.
This is Irish dancing. The girls are
hopping on one leg.

Irish dancers

This is the Hopak dance. The men are kicking their legs.

Hopak dancers

This boy isn't dancing with
other people.

Lots of people watch dance shows.

In the street

They watch dancers in the street, at the theatre and on television.

On television

In a theatre

These children are dancing on the beach.

These children are dancing in the playground.

Where do you like to dance?

Why do you dance?

Picture dictionary

Listen and repeat

dancing

hopping

kicking

street

television

theatre

1 Look and match

ballet   Hopak

carnival   Zumba

2 Listen and say

Download a reading guide for parents and teachers at
www.collins.co.uk/839687

Collins

Published by Collins
An imprint of HarperCollins*Publishers*
Westerhill Road
Bishopbriggs
Glasgow
G64 2QT

HarperCollins*Publishers*
1st Floor, Watermarque Building
Ringsend Road
Dublin 4
Ireland

William Collins' dream of knowledge for all began with the publication of his first book in 1819.

A self-educated mill worker, he not only enriched millions of lives, but also founded a flourishing publishing house. Today, staying true to this spirit, Collins books are packed with inspiration, innovation and practical expertise. They place you at the centre of a world of possibility and give you exactly what you need to explore it.

© HarperCollins*Publishers* Limited 2020

10 9 8 7 6 5 4 3 2

ISBN 978-0-00-839687-9

Collins® and COBUILD® are registered trademarks of HarperCollins*Publishers* Limited

www.collins.co.uk/elt

All rights reserved. No part of this publication may be reproduced, stored in a retrieval system, or transmitted in any form by any means, electronic, mechanical, photocopying, recording or otherwise, without the prior written permission of the Publisher or a licence permitting restricted copying in the United Kingdom issued by the Copyright Licensing Agency Ltd, 5th Floor, Shackleton House, 4 Battle Bridge Lane, London SE1 2HX.

British Library Cataloguing in Publication Data

A catalogue record for this publication is available from the British Library.

All rights reserved. No part of this book may be reproduced, stored in a retrieval system, or transmitted in any form or by any means, electronic, mechanical, photocopying, recording or otherwise, without the prior permission in writing of the Publisher. This book is sold subject to the conditions that it shall not, by way of trade or otherwise, be lent, re-sold, hired out or otherwise circulated without the Publisher's prior consent in any form of binding or cover other than that in which it is published and without a similar condition including this condition being imposed on the subsequent purchaser.

Author: Sarah Jane Lewis-Mantzaris
Illustrator: Jan Smith (Beehive)
Series editor: Rebecca Adlard
Commissioning editor: Zoë Clarke
Publishing manager: Lisa Todd
Product managers: Jennifer Hall and Caroline Green
In-house editor: Alma Puts Keren
Project manager: Emily Hooton
Editor: Tessie Papadopoulou-Dalton
Proofreaders: Natalie Murray and Michael Lamb
Cover designer: Kevin Robbins
Typesetter: 2Hoots Publishing Services Ltd
Audio produced by id audio, London
Reading guide author: Emma Wilkinson
Production controller: Rachel Weaver
Printed and bound by: GPS Group, Slovenia

MIX
Paper from
responsible sources
FSC™ C007454

This book is produced from independently certified FSC™ paper to ensure responsible forest management.

For more information visit: **www.harpercollins.co.uk/green**

Download the audio for this book and a reading guide for parents and teachers at www.collins.co.uk/839687